BULLS

Curious Kids Press

Bulls

A bull is a male in the cattle species that is still able to reproduce. There are around 800 breeds of cattle. This animal belongs to the Ungulate family and the more commonly known subfamily of the Bovine. Cattle have been domesticated and live on farms or ranches and are kept mostly for their meat and hides. There is so much more to learn about bulls, so let's get started and explore the fascinating world of this huge animal.

Where in the World?

Did you know there are around 1.3 billion cattle on the planet? Cattle and the bulls can be found in most places around the world. They were thought to be first domesticated (tamed) around 10,500 years-ago in southeast Turkey. Most species today came from as few as 80 individuals from the past.

The Body of a Bull

Did you know a bull is a huge animal? Depending on the species, bulls can weigh from 2,000 to 3,300 pounds! They have shorter legs with hooves, a long tail and a very stocky body. Their heads are large and some even have horns. Their eyes are very small in comparison to the rest of their head.

The Bull's Fur

Did you know that some leather products are made from cattle skin? The bull's and other cattle skin is use to make products like shoes, purses and coats. The fur on a bull is very coarse and kind of prickly to the touch. Bulls can come in many different colors and some even have patterns on their coats.

The Bull's Horns

Did you know the horns on a bull are very dangerous? The bull uses its hard sharp horns to defend itself and members of the herd. The horns on a bull are called true horns. Over top of the bony horns are pieces of skin that are made up of keratin and proteins.

A Bull's Powerful Sport

Did you know bulls are extremely powerful? The Spanish bull is used in a "sport" called, bullfighting. This is where an angry bull is let loose in a ring with a matador. This person uses a cape to fool the bull into running at him. The bulls are very strong and could kill the matador if given the chance.

A Bull's Cud

Did you know the bull chews its cud? Like all of the cattle species, bulls have 4 chambers in their stomach. One of these chambers holds unchewed food called, cud. After the bull has eaten grass or hay, it will bring it back up in its mouth to chew it. The bull can do this for hours on end.

The Bull's Senses

Did you know the bull uses all 5 of his senses? Bulls use taste, touch, sound, sight and smell to go through life. However, its sense of smell and sight are the strongest. He can detect smells from 5 miles away and also when a female is ready to mate. His eyesight can see 360 degrees and he can see all colors except red.

The Bull as Prey

Did you know bulls have few natural predators? Large carnivores like cougars, bears and wolves will hunt cattle, but the bull is usually not one of them. Since the bull is very strong and fierce, carnivores would rather hunt a female or a smaller member of the herd. However, bulls will protect the members of his herd.

Bull Talk

Did you know the bull can communicate? We have all learned that cattle say moo, but they can also make other sounds, too. Bulls will grunt, snort and even make a low growling sound when they feel threatened or around a female cow. They can also bawl quite loudly and make a bellowing sound.

Father Bull

Did you know the bull lives with several females? Among a herd of cattle, there is usually one bull. His job is to protect the herd and to impregnate the females (cows). His herd is called a, harem. After the bull is finished mating with the female, he leaves the cow to raise the calf.

Baby Bull

Did you know it takes 9 months for a baby bull to be born? Once the calf is born it will suckle from its mother. The baby bull is not very strong for the first week of its life. The cow will keep her baby bull hidden until he is strong enough to keep up with the herd.

Life of a Bull

Did you know bulls can live to be around 28 years-old? Bulls can live for a long time, but some species will get very aggressive at around 4 to 5 years-old. Since humans use cattle as a source of meat and for products, many bulls do not make it to adulthood.

Ankole Bull

This species of bull is native to Africa. It has huge thick horns that can reach spans of 8 feet wide from tip to tip. This bull can be light to dark brown in color and weigh up to 1,600 pounds. It is found on the savannas and open grasslands where it grazes on grass and leaves.

Texas Longhorn

As the name suggests, this bull is found in Texas. It has very long horns that extend up and out from its head. These horns can measure over 7 feet wide from tip to tip. This bull can come in a variety of colors, but dark red and white are the most common. Bulls of this breed are very smart.

Quiz

Question 1: What species is the bull a male of?

Answer 1: Cattle

Question 2: How big can a bull grow?

Answer 2: Up to 3,300 pounds!

Question 3: What is the skin made up of that covers the bull's horns?

Answer 3: Keratin and proteins

Question 4: From what distance can a male detect a female?

Answer 4: Up to 5 miles away

Question 5: The bull has many females in his herd. What is this called?

Answer 5: His harem

Thank you for checking out another addition from Curious Kids Press! Make sure to check out Amazon.com for many other great titles.